The MTM Party*Print Guide

NICOLE GATES

authorHOUSE®

AuthorHouse™
1663 Liberty Drive, Suite 200
Bloomington, IN 47403
www.authorhouse.com
Phone: 1-800-839-8640

First published by AuthorHouse   9/11/2008

ISBN: 978-1-4343-9804-8 (sc)

Printed in the United States of America
Bloomington, Indiana

This book is printed on acid-free paper.

TABLE OF CONTENTS

The Love's of My Life!

My Lord & Savior who has instilled in me that I CAN DO ALL THINGS...through HIM!

My Family who through thick and thin have been supportive even when they thought my rhyme had no reason.

My daughters Yolanda, Savanna, Brooklyn & Bheanna...you have all inspired me to be the Woman, Mother & Businesswoman that I am. I hope that one day you will appreciate all my hard work and creativity! I love you and encourage you to strive towards your dreams!

Devon, who have always been my creative consultants and guinea pig over the years. I thank you for your support in all of my endeavors.

My granddaughter Cheyenne who will someday become my little helper! Hint! Hint!

My dearest friend Emmanuel your words of wisdom, love and support has inspired me to reach a new plateau giving me a desire to press forward and not settle!

My G.E.M.S. (God's Evidence Manifested in SISTAhood) who have all in one way or another assisted in making me a well-rounded person! My Pearl- Yolanda Tate, Ruby- Latonya Benson, Amethyst- Krista Gibson, Sapphire- Doris Lee, Blue Topaz- Sandy Williams, Emerald- Tracy White & Onyx- Tamesha Bernard. You ladies shed bright light on a place that once was dim and dark! God Bless You All!

My Passion to PARTY!

Have a passion to entertain, but dread the thought of hosting a party? Sometimes entertaining can become cumbersome to a mom who wears a million different hats a day, but the benefits of hosting a party outweigh the stress. I, too, am a busy mother (of four) with a career, but I have this undying passion to entertain. Not just to entertain, but to entertain my guests to the point that they leave salivating for my next get-together!

I started off using excuses for gatherings, like "Oh, Christmas is coming! Let's throw a little Christmas Eve party." After planning and hosting the get-togethers and seeing my guests enjoying themselves and raving over the food, keepsakes, and decor, I found that I received some type of adrenaline rush that kept me floating for days. So I started planning parties just for fun.

Recently I became known as the "Queen of Theme," as I love to host parties with very unusual themes. I think of a reason to have a get-together, look for a theme, plan the menu (depending on the theme, the menu may become elaborate), design and create appropriate invitations and a thank-you keepsake for all of my guests (I love giving my guests something to remember our theme for the night), and transform my party space to accommodate the theme.

I have hosted holiday buffet parties, Polynesian paradise parties, spa parties, an all-pink birthday party for my twin girls' first birthday, a taste of Tunica (casino night) party, a make-your-own Martini party, an all-star jam celebration, and more!

I am sure it has crossed your mind that you don't have the time to plan and execute such events, let alone the energy, so here are some of my tips:

- If you are fortunate enough to have kids around, solicit their help. Kids want to help, especially when it comes to partying!

- If you're not sure of a theme, search the Internet and look through magazines — there are themes all around you.

- When planning a menu, use quick and easy recipes or purchase ready-made food from your favorite store.

- The highlight of your shindig should be the impression that has been left with your guests. Think of a really unique keepsake that they would be pleased to leave with. These can be very inexpensive — all you have to do is be creative in what you choose or how you dress it up.

- Don't stress yourself out. Plan ahead. Let your ideas flow. Then map out your plan and execute it!

To Whom Much Is Given
Much Is Required

By Krista S. Webb-Gibson

Have you ever heard it said to whom much is given much is required?
There is no limit to this and it never expires. Everyone should be careful not
to boast in themselves, Or forget from what direction they too received help.
We give and receive things many times hoping that no strings are attached.
But when it comes to God's giving there's no gift that can ever be matched.
Some people give things only wanting to receive something fleshly in return.
God's only requirement is that for him your soul will yearn. Gifts that
given individually to us are not to be used for our own selfish purpose.
But to reach out to others and direct them to Him is why He chose
in us to birth this. Reaching out to others does not require that you
constantly point out their flaws or faults. First start by working with the
person in the mirror and stop premeditating verbal assaults. Yes, I too
believe that to whom much is given much is required. Take your eyes
off yourself, reach out to someone else and we all will go a little higher.

PARTY*PRINT

Main Entry: par: typrint

Pronounication: partE "print

1. A detailed plan of action to execute the ultimate theme event
   or social gathering.

It's Your Turn...Get Inspired!

Nothing can be great without PASSION!

The most creative of themes will come from a concept that houses tiers that allow you to fortify the theme through the décor, menu, invitations, color scheme, drinks and music.

The MTM Party*Print Guide was designed with you in mind! We have implemented some creative themes that will allow you opportunities to entertain and make sure your guests leave with *More than A Memory*!

Let's get started...

Have you set a date? Have you picked a theme? Have you thought about your WOW factor? Ok, don't fret! Let's take a closer look to see what the guide has to offer! Put on your creative thinking caps and let's begin our journey!

Chocolate Cocktail Party

Party Theme Description

A Chocolate Lover's Heaven this party offers an intriguingly decadent alternative to the traditional cocktail party!

Party Tips/ Planning Stages

Invitations

- Send guests their invites on the wrapper of a chocolate candy bar

Keepsakes

- Make chocolate goody bags for all guests, try to pick chocolates that are unique, i.e. personalized chocolate bars, personalized chocolate pops, etc.
- Chocolate Candy Roses for the Ladies

Party Activities

Chocolate Trivia

- Ask guests to name all of the companies and types of chocolate known to them. Award the winner a extra-large Hershey Kiss.

Party Food Ideas

- Double Chocolate Cheesecake
- Tortillas Dulce
- Decadent Chocolate Mousse
- Grand Marnier Honey Chocolate Fondue w/ladyfingers and pound cake
- Chocolate Pound Cake
- Cocoa-Crusted Shrimp w/ Basil

- Mochatini
- Banana Split-ini
- Flaming Alexander

Party Drinks
- Hot Chocolate with a Twist
- Champagne
- Dry Riesling (Erorica, Leasingham Bin7 or Ars Vitis)

CHOCOLATE TASTING PARTY

Party Theme Description	Giving Chocolate tasting parties for birthdays, anniversaries, showers and other occasions where chocolate would enhance the event
Party Tips	Research how chocolate is made—from bean to bar. Share with your guests.
	Get 10-12 of your favorite kinds of chocolate so you'll have enough variety to compare or contrast.
	Make labels for each plate so guests know what they are biting into.
	Have pretzels on hand to cleanse the palates of between chocolates.
	Create your own chocolate tasting score cards with a simple rating scale so that guests will have a record of what they liked or disliked.
Party Keepsakes	Use festive gable boxes and provide each guest one of each of your favorite chocolates…maybe even include a recipe that uses this type of chocolate.
Party Drinks	Try pairing the chocolates to some of your favorite wines. A great choice would be the

Chocolate Trivia

Okay, I love chocolate and for many years had heard that chocolate was an aphrodisiac. NOT!! Here's the facts...

Did you know?

- Chocolate contains phenyl ethylamine (PEA), a natural substance that stimulates the body and causes it to have the same reaction as falling in love!

- We spend more than $7 billion a year on chocolate, More than $1 billion between Thanksgiving and New Years.

- Although the cocoa butter in chocolate is high in saturated fats, it has not been known to raise blood cholesterol.

- U.S. chocolate lovers eat about 2.8 billion pounds of chocolate a year.

- Chocolate syrup was used for blood in the classic Alfred Hitchcock movie "Psycho"

- Chocolate has over 500 flavor components

- There are 5 to 10 milligrams of caffeine in one ounce of bittersweet chocolate, 5 milligrams in milk chocolate and 10 milligrams in a 6 ounce cup of cocoa.

- Chocolate has been said to be a wonderful source of energy.

Fondue Fantasy

Party Description

- Retro, fun, cool and funky fondue cooking is fast, convenient and very trendy. Whether entertaining friends or having a family dinner, fondue can take you from tasty appetizer and flavorful main dish to luscious dessert.

- "Fondue" comes from the French word "fon-dre," meaning "to melt."

Party Tips/ Planning Stages

- "Look at the wine against a white background--take the glass and tilt it against a white napkin or a piece of paper

- "If the color isn't brown, move on, "Then you're on to the scent. To maximize that, give the glass a swirl.

- Stick your nose into the glass and inhale. "Go ahead and give it a smell. What you want first is for the wine to be in good condition--not vinegary, not musty.

- Only now do you taste.

- Feel the wine in your mouth to evaluate its body.

- Finally, savor the aftertaste--or what professionals call the finish.

- We all know that white wine is served cold and red wine at room temperature, but there are many subtleties to serving wine.

Party Food Ideas

- **Cheese fondue** - is a mouth-watering mixture of easy-to-melt cheeses, like GruyÄ¨re or Edam, blended with a dry, white wine. The velvety, smooth sauce is perfect for dipping bread cubes or raw vegetables.

- **Sizzling fondue** - is a hot-oil mixture in which you cook skewered pieces of raw beef or seafood, then dip the juicy morsels into one or more savory, seasoned sauces. A lighter version of this fondue uses heated broth rather than oil.

- **Chocolate fondue** - combines melted bittersweet or semisweet chocolate with heavy cream, peanut butter or coconut. Into this heavenly confection, you can swirl large chunks of brownies, pound cake, biscotti or seasonal fresh fruits such as strawberries, bananas, cherries, grapes or peaches.

Party Food Ideas

Before you get started, remember these fondue tips:

- Prepare the fondue on the stovetop first, then transfer the mixture to the fondue pot.

- Remove the dipped morsel from the fondue and place it on your plate.

- Don't try to eat directly from the fondue fork because they can get extremely hot.

- Keep the fondue pot no more than one-third to one-half filled with the melted cheese, chocolate or hot oil.

- Protect your tabletop by placing the fondue pot on a sturdy trivet.

If you ever wanted to get in on a fad, this is the one. Try these easy recipes and get started today. But, remember, no double dipping!

Fondue Favorites

Grand Marnier-Honey Chocolate Fondue

1 c bittersweet chocolate, melted
1 c semi-sweet chocolate, melted
½ c heavy cream
2 tsp. orange zest
Pinch of Salt
2 tbsp. honey
¼ c Grand Marnier

Assorted fresh fruit, cut into bite-sized pieces, as needed Ladyfingers or pound cake, cut into bite-sized pieces, as needed

Directions:

1. Combine the melted chocolates and keep warm.

2. Bring the heavy cream, orange zest, salt and honey to a simmer. Remove from heat and allow the zest to steep 5 minutes. Strain the mixture into the chocolate and whisk together.

3. Add the Grand Marnier and mix thoroughly. Serve warm in a fondue pot with a variety of foods to dip.

For white chocolate fondue, substitute 2 c melted white chocolate for the bittersweet and semi-sweet chocolate.

MTM Chocolate Strawberry Fondue

2 tsp. butter

2 c milk chocolate morsels, melted

½ c cool whip

¼ c Tequila Rose Cocoa Cream

Directions:

1. Melt chocolate and keep warm
2. Add cool whip and butter
3. Whisk together
4. Add Tequila Rose Cocoa Cream
5. Mix thoroughly, mixture should be smooth
6. Serve warm in a fondue pot

Serve with strawberries, orange segments, cake chunks, bananas, pineapple, pretzels, granny smith apples, etc.

For a more decadent treat… dip in chocolate then in ground walnuts or pecans.

POLYNESIAN PARADISE

Party Theme Description

Hosting a Polynesian Paradise party, celebrates the festive fun, food and flair of Hawaiian culture.

Party Tips/ Planning Stages

Décor

- create a traditional center table runner of leaves, ferns and flowers or you can go with an ocean theme and spread an ornamental fishnet topped with shells, sand and glass balls
- Raffia hula skirts look tropical edging the buffet table

Keepsakes

- You could pack little take out cartons of chocolate-covered macadamia nuts for party favors

Party Activities

- Hula Hoop Contest
- Limbo

Finger Food Buffet

- BBQ Quesadillas
- Cheese Quesadillas w/ Guacamole

Party Food Ideas

- Cocktail Meatballs
- Deviled Eggs
- Louisiana Crab Cakes w/Corn relish
- Rum Glazed Shrimp

The Mai Tai

1 ounce Light Rum
1 ounce Coruba or Red Heart Jamaican Rum
1/2 ounce French Orgeat
1/2 ounce Orange Curacao
1/4 ounce Rock Candy Syrup

Party Drinks   Juice of one fresh lime
Orange juice

Fill a large 15 ounce glass with ingredients,
then add crushed ice and splash of orange
juice. Garnish with mint leaves, pineapple slice
and for a real tropical look add an orchid and
a miniature paper parasol!

Creating a Polynesian Paradise

Polynesians are known to be very warm and hospitable people. A nice way to welcome your guests is to offer them some beautiful tropical flower leis and a authentic tropical cocktail. Learn some native Polynesian lingo to share with guests... have the words and their meanings posted around the venue. Ensure that your venue is festively decorated with beautiful floral arrangements, tikis and Polynesian table settings, etc. Prepare foods that coincide with the theme of the party.

How to Make Polynesian Tropical Flower Leis

Materials
Tropical flowers (hibiscus, tiares, or frangipanis)
White colored thread
Needle
Scissors

Step 1:
Measure the size of your flower leis by placing the thread around your neck

Step 2:
Using the thread and needle, pierce straight through the middle of the flower. Continue until you feel you have enough flowers on the thread.

Step 3:
Holding the two ends of the thread, allow some space to tie a knot.

You can have a variety of tropical flowers on one leis...NO LIMITS!

STRAWBERRIES, SALSA & SANGRIAS

Party Theme Description	Tapas are appetizers that usually accompany sangrias or other appetizers and festive cocktails. Tapas have become trendy foods for fun and festive celebrations.

Décor

Party Tips/ Planning Stages	• Enchantment by candlelight... a combination of floating candles and fresh fruit slices or floating candles and orchid blossoms to create flavorful centerpieces

Turn the music up; let your hair down and SALSA!

Party Activities	• Give express Salsa lessons… Don't know how to Salsa?
	• Hire a Dance Instructor or Enthusiast to teach you and your guest how.

Party Food Ideas

- Meat-filled Empanadas
- Fruit Tapas
- Meat-filled Tapas
- Seafood Tapas
- Banana Quesadillas
- Fruit Salsa
- Chocolate Chipotle Brownies
- Salsa Borracha

Party Drinks

Sangria is a traditional beverage that combines red wine and fruit.

- Red Wine Sangria
- White Wine Sangria
- Prosecco Sangria
- Rose Sangria
- Prickly Pear Sangria

MTM Salsa & Sangrias Favorites

Mango Salsa

2 c diced Mango
½ c minced red onion
½ c minced red bell pepper
2 tsp. jalapeno pepper
¼ c lime juice
¼ c chopped cilantro

Mix all ingredients and splash to taste with slat and pepper.
Refrigerate for up to three days.

Pomegranate Sangria

18 oz. POM Wonderful Pomegranate Juice
1 750 ml. bottle of dry, fruity white wine
6 oz. apricot brandy
6 oz. cream sherry
1 oz. simple syrup
1 oz. Sparkling Wine
1 lime, sliced into wheels
1 lemon, sliced into wheels
½ orange, sliced into wheels
½ grapefruit, sliced into wheels

Garnish

Red apple wedges, Green apple wedges, orange wedges, grapefruit wedges, Cava Spanish Sparkling Brut

1. Place all ingredients into a sangria pitcher

2. Refrigerate and let stand 2 hours before serving

3. For an individual serving, pour sangria over ice top with fruit garnish

4. Finish each serving with a splash of Cava Spanish Sparkling Brut

Make Your Own Martini Party

Party Theme Description

- Time to shake things up! Martini Parties are the perfect alternative to the classic cocktail party. Out with the classic Martini... Welcome some flavor to your party!

Party Tips/ Planning Stages

- Ask each guest to bring one item from the list you make to set up your Martini Bar... make sure you have enough to make a variety of drinks.

Party Activities

- Ask guest to compete in making the ultimate Martini, guests can create based on what ingredients are available... Give drink shakers to winners.
- Ask all guests to submit their favorite martini recipe and combine to create a Martini Recipe Book for a keepsake.

Hors d'oeuvres are little gifts that entice your guest's taste buds.

Party Food Ideas

- Swedish Meatballs
- Cocktail Meatballs
- Turkey Meatballs
- Mozzarella Bites
- Jalapeño Poppers
- Fried Oysters
- Mini Chicken Kebobs
- Mini Burger Bite Kebobs

Sangria is a traditional beverage that combines red wine and fruit.

Blood Orange Martini

Party Drinks

4 ounces vodka
1/2 ounce triple sec or flavored orange liqueur
2 ounces blood orange juice
2 blood orange slices

In a martini shaker combine all ingredients except the orange slices with a generous amount of ice. Shake vigorously for a few seconds. Strain the libation from the ice into a martini glass. Garnish with the orange slices.

The Mystery of the Martini

A Martini is a cocktail containing unequal portions of gin and dry vermouth (in a ratio of somewhere between 2:1 and 15:1, inclusive) served chilled, in a conical stemmed glass, garnished with either a green olive or a lemon twist.

Try these MTM Favorites:

Mojito Martini

3 parts Bacardi Limon
2 parts Sprite
1 part Sweet & Sour Mix

Serve in a chilled Martini glass.

Cherry Cheesecake

1 part Vanilla Schnapps
1 splash cream
1 splash Cranberry Juice

Serve in a chilled Martini glass.

Dreamsicle Martini

1 part Stoli Gold Vodka
1 part Dry Vermouth
1 part Sweet Vermouth
1 splash Orange Juice

Serve in a chilled Martini glass

Berry Berry Martini

2 part Raspberry Vodka
1 part Raspberry Liqueur
Splash of Cranberry Juice

Serve in a chilled Martini glass.

Apple Cinnamon Martini

1 part Grey Goose Vodka
2 parts Apple Pucker
½ part Cinnamon Schnapps

Garnish with a slice of a red apple or cinnamon stick

Serve in a chilled Martini glass.

Amateur Wine Tasting

Party Theme Description

Just about anytime is a perfect time to enjoy a wine tasting event. The amateur wine tasting allows you to learn the wines you prefer while challenging your guests to choose their favorites.

Party Tips/Planning Stages

Plan the Wine Tasting... offer six wines and six tasters (guests).

Each taster will need a separate glass for each wine. A party this size will need 36 wine glasses.

Inform your guests of the types of wines (red, white or rose).

Ask each guest to bring a wine from one of the three categories... try not to duplicate.

Conceal bottles in wine bags and place color-coded toppers to each bottle. Try to find matching glass charms for the glasses.

Provide each guest a sample of the wine…be sure to pour the wine with matching topper & charms in the glasses. Glasses should be one third of a glass for each sample.

Tasting begins with your guests examining the color. Taking not of its clarity. Write down what you observe.

Smell the wine. Place your hand over the bowl of your glass and gently swirl. This aerates the wine and releases its aromas.

Tasting

Taste the wine. Allow the wine to sit in your mouth for a few seconds before swallowing. Understand that different areas of the mouth are sensitive to a different aspect of taste.

Rank the wine. One being the best.

Vote on the wine. Have a stack of color coded disks. As host/hostess you will begin the voting process by taking a bag and asking each guest to enter the colored-coded disk in the bag that they rated one, two and so on.

Unveil the wine. Add suspense by revealing the worst to first. Each taster now has the opportunity to hang their head or hold it high!

KNOW YOUR WINES

What to Red Wines?

Hearty, full bodied, dry
Deep crimson to purple, reddish-orange or rust
Not refrigerated, served at 60-65° F
Served very lightly chilled

Red Wines by Name

Cabernet Sauvignon	Cassis, Blackberry, Cherry, Mint, Cedar, Herbs
Pinot Noir	Strawberry, Cherry, Violets, Spices
Merlot	Berry, Plum, Cherry, Spices
Zinfandel	Blackberry, Raspberry, Black Pepper
Syrah	
Shiraz	
Grenach Blanc	
Gamay Beaujolais	
Mourvedre	
Tempranillo	
Sangionese	
Chianti	
Nebbiolo	
Barolo	
Lambrusco	

What to White Wines?

Pale straw, to bright yellow to gold
More delicate
Ranges from very dry to sweet
Served chilled or fully refrigerated

White Wines by Name/Bouquet

Chardonnay   Pineapple, Pear, Green Apple, Citrus, Butter,
                      Nuts, Spices

Chablis

Sauvignon Blanc   Grapefruit, Lemon, Floral Notes, Melon, Dry
                      Herbs, Bell Pepper, Butter

Graves

Riesling

Chenin Blanc

Gewurztraminer

Alberino

Pinot Blanc

Pinot Grigio… a.k.a. Marsanne or Pinot Gris

Muscat

Muller-Thurgau

Wine Pairing Guide

Cabernet Sauvignon
> Beef, Lamb Chops, Roast, Wine-based sauces, Chocolate

Beaujolais'
> Chicken & Turkey

Sparkling Wines
> Caviar, Oysters, Cold Shellfish, Fruit

Chardonnay
> Fish, Chinese Food

Pinot Blanc
> Fish, Chinese Food

Merlot
> Sharp cheeses, Lamb, Pork Chops

Pinot Noir
> Tuna, Swordfish, Roasted Chicken, Turkey

Super Tuscan
> Prosucitto, Pasta, Meats

Chianti
> Pasta, Italian Food, Proscuitto

Sauvignon Blanc
> Fish, Chinese Food

Zinfandel
> Barbeque

Sunset Safari Party

Party Theme Description

Party kicks off at Sunset! Enjoy a night of festivities and great safari fun when you host this theme party!

Party Tips/ Planning Stages

- Use bamboo placemats, tabletops tiki torches and plenty of animal prints to set the tone of this event.
- Find safari instrumental music, play during the party to add to the ambiance
- Look for unique coconut shaped cups or canteens to serve drinks
- Try hanging inflatable monkeys from an artificial palm tree in a corner of the room

Invitations

- Prepare invitations on a label and apply to a paper compass for your guests, give directions that include the words *North, South, East & West.*

Party Activities

Keepsakes

- Safari Survival Trail Mix
- Personalized Back Scratchers
- Personal Portable Fans

Guests

- Ask each guest to wear cargo pants, shorts & safari shirts

Party Activities (cont.)

- Encourage guests to go the whole nine yards by bringing their own Canteen, Bug Spray, Suntan Lotion, etc.

Activity

- Prepare a scavenger hunt for guests to participate in as teams or as individuals

- Mango Salsa & Elephant Ears (Restaurant Style Tortilla Chips)

- Grilled Chicken with Mango Salsa

- Wild Berry and Basil Salad

- Caramelized Bananas w/ & Vanilla Ice

Party Food Ideas

- Pulled Wild Boar (Pork) w/ Tamarind Sauce on Kaiser Rolls

- Safari Packs...Pulled Pork & Coleslaw served in a Pita

- Fruit Spears-An array of fresh fruit on bamboo skewers

- Monkey Bread

- Safari Sunset

- Safari Sangrias

- Mango Monkey

Party Drinks

2 oz. Grey Goose Vodka
¾ oz. Triple Sec
2 oz. Mango juice or nectar
½ frozen banana, in cubes
1 ice cube

Add all ingredients into a blender and puree. Pour into a wine or other large stemmed glass. Garnish with a mango wedge.

PICASSO PARTY

Party Theme Description

The Picasso Party is a great idea for birthdays. Especially the birthdays of multiples! Encourage the little Picasso in your child/children!

Party Tips/ Planning Stages

I absolutely love Crayola….they always provide us as parents new innovative ideas in art and creativity! I highly recommend using their products.

Purchase Crayola's mess free products… Color Wonder Fingerpaints, Erasables, Twistables, Color Explosion and Washable Crayons, Markers and Paints!

Purchase plastic tablecloths that can be cut in half to use as drop cloths for each Creation Station.

Party Activities

Provide Picasso Creation Stations
Some Ideas…

- Make Your Own Bubble Gum Machine
- Create A Shirt
- Design Your Own Art Box
- Design Your Own Frameable Art

Visit www.michaels.com/art/online or www. crayola.com for more Creation Station Ideas~

Party Keepsakes

For each guest that attends the Picasso Party… send them home with their very own Picasso Art Kit, complete with crayons, coloring pad, colored pencils, etc.

Hearts of Virtue

Mother/Daughter Retreat

"A true friend is one who knows you as you really are,
understands where you've been, accepts who you've become, and
still gently invites you to grow"

Party Theme Description	The Hearts of Virtue Mother/Daughter Retreat embraces the idea that older women should train and prepare the younger women, based on the principles Titus 2:3-4.
Party Tips/ Planning Stages	Identify Mothers and Daughters that would benefit from an afternoon of spiritual fellowship. Invite them to share in an afternoon tea.
Party Activities	Ask Mothers to pick a woman from the Bible and read her story. Ask her to present at the tea how she compares to the woman that she chose. Some examples of Women in the Bible: Deborah, Esther, Abigail, Sarah, Hannah, Priscilla, Lydia, Tabitha, Joanna, Mary, Martha, etc.

Party Activities (cont.)	The Sea of Adolescence- Mothers and Daughters meet in separate groups and talk about some of the potential obstacles to positive communication in the adolescent years. Then compare lists, leading to an interesting discussion between generations about the means to grow up and what kind of support girls need.

Make A Wish- Another game that is both fun and challenging involves each mother and daughter making a private/public wish and/or desire for the future. |
| **Party Keepsakes** | Hearts of Virtue Hope Chest with a variety of inspirational and spiritual items. |

Book Exchange

Party Theme Description

A great idea for a just because party. The Book exchange can be enjoyed by all! Help your child enjoy reading and why not share this experience with other parents of children!

Party Tips/ Planning Stages

- Send invites on bookmarks to all invited guests.
- If you know of a local author, try to get them to come and support your event. Maybe include a book signing so each child can receive their very own autographed book.
- Have children dress as their favorite book character.
- Display your favorite books around the room.
- How about decorating the party room like a scene from your favorite book!
- Give all guests that attend bookmarks, a journal, pencils/pens that will encourage them to write about their favorite books.

Party Activities

- Create a guest list of family and friends who have children that are approx. the same age as the children that will be participating. This will ensure that books are age appropriate.
- Ask guests to go through their books at home and fill a box with the ones that they no longer read and may be ready to replace

**Party Food
Ideas**

- Try serving foods that are found in some of your children's favorite books.

- Have a variety of kid-friendly foods.

- Pint size milk, juice, etc.

Movie Night

**Party Theme
Description**

- Test your movie knowledge! A great way to celebrate your love for movies! Turn your party pad into a private theater by hosting a movie/tv night!

**Party Tips/
Planning Stages**

- For fun, lay down a red carpet, or try a few feet of inexpensive LED rope light along seating rows to delineate different sections.
- Go to your local Movie Theatre and ask for old movie posters/memorabilia to decorate your party space.

Party Activities

- Spice up your movie/tv night by asking your guests to write reviews for their favorite.
- Guess the Actor/Actress- on labels write the name of the Actor/Actress, place one on the back of each guest- ask guests to guess who they are.

- For a more casual night, why not kick your favorite concession stand classics up a notch? Popcorn, candy, and hot dogs are great alternatives to a fancy, four-star meal. And nothing goes better with the big screen than a huge ice cream soda.

- Strawberry Ice-Cream Sodas

Party Food Ideas
- Top your own Popcorn (Cheese, Spicy, Chocolate)

- Classic Chicago Style Hotdog

- Corn Dogs

- Party Pizza (all the toppings)

- Concession Snacks (Raisinettes, Reece's, Twizzler's, etc.)

Holiday Brunch

Party Theme Description	A festive mid-morning affair. The perfect way to ring in the holidays.
Party Tips/Planning Stages	Decorations for the holidays make this a perfect time for entertaining.
Party Activities	Create a holiday puzzle with a picture you have mounted and cut into as many pieces as you have guests. Have everyone try to put the puzzle together. Play holiday trivia by making up questions about holiday movies, traditions, etc. Some guests may have questions while others may have answers. Play holiday music in the background.
Party Food Ideas	Coffee (flavored or regular), tea (herbal and breakfast), juice, Mimosas, Bloody Mary's, bagels, cream cheese, muffins, breakfast pastries, variety of quiches, spiral ham, potato salad, fruit salad, cheese platter, cream/milk, sugar, butter

Holiday Party Guide

Plan Ahead

- Get ready for holiday house guests... get your house in order! Have plenty of household items on hand.
- Finalize your menus and make your grocery shopping list... make a list of meals that you will prepare and things you'll need
- Spruce up your table

Keep It Simple

- Lights! Cameras! ACTION!- Set the mood with celebratory lights
- Music- Music is one of the most important element to the party atmosphere
- Décor- Keep your theme in mind and play it all the way through! Be as creative as possible.
- Food Fetes- Serve easy to handle and easy to prepare foods that are scrumptious!

Relax & Enjoy

- A good host knows how to relax and feel like a guest at their own party!
- Prepare these simple crowd pleasers ahead of time and you're sure to enjoy.

Tips to Impress Your Guest

- Serve with Style- use festive serving dishes bowls, spoons, and a variety of platters and decorative spreaders.

- Creatively present dishes & snacks- use a variety of shaped dishes and colors to create a unique setting.

How to Conduct a

White Elephant Gift Exchange

White elephant gift exchange (also called Yankee Swap, Thieving Secret Santa, Nasty Christmas, Dirty Santa, Scrooge's Christmas, Chinese Gift Exchange, Chinese auction, or Thieving Elves) is a popular party game usually played during the Christmas season. The premise of the game is that each guest contributes one gift to the game, and ultimately each guest walks away with one different gift from the game. Gifts can be decided on ahead of time.

All participants bring their gift to "the pile." Gifts are wrapped, but are not labeled to reflect a sender or recipient. In some variants the gift is even wrapped inside-out so that the printed part of the wrapping paper is not visible to the recipient. Gifts are typically inexpensive, humorous items; the term white elephant refers to a gift whose cost exceeds its usefulness.

All participants draw a number to determine their order. The participant with #1 unwraps any gift from the pile and then shows it to everyone. Each successive participant, in the order determined from the drawing, can either...

1) "steal" an already opened gift (if there's one they really like)

2) be adventurous and go for a wrapped gift from the pile.

Note: If the participant chooses to steal, the person whose gift is stolen now repeats their turn and either

1) steals another person's gift (they cannot immediately steal back the gift that was just stolen from them)

2) unwraps a new gift. This cycle of stealing can sometimes continue for a long time, until a new gift is chosen, at which point the turn is passed to the participant with the next number from the drawing.

Since items can be stolen, the item in your possession is not yours until the game is over (i.e. a food item cannot be eaten until the game is over).

However, this is often amended with a rule declaring a gift "dead" or "safe" after it has been stolen a certain number of times (usually two or three).

This helps the process go more smoothly and limits the disadvantage of being among the first to choose gifts.

Cutting Edge Cocktail Party

Party Theme Description	Embrace the old while experimenting with the new! This Cutting Edge Cocktail Party is a trendy alternative to the retro cocktail party.
Party Tips/ Planning Stages	• Instead of hiding alcohol's flavor choose a cocktail that you can highlight the alcohol. • Use 3-4 ingredients per drink for better flavor • Serve drinks in smaller glasses • Make drinks in batches beforehand
Party Activities	• Conduct a food pairing to your favorite cocktails • Flavor Your Own Spirit Contest- Ask guests to experiment and infuse their favorite spirits, bring to the party along with a recipe that they'll share with others. • Make Your Own House-Made Bitters & Sweet & Sour Mixers
Party Food Ideas	A sophisticated adult gathering fueled by mixed drinks and finger foods, the perfect antidote to the classic cocktail party.

Party Drinks

Comebacks- Stirred Drinks & Cocktails made prior to prohibition

- White Lady
- Mint Julep
- Gimlets
- Mai Tais

New to the Scene

- Flavored Mojitos
- Cachaca
- Martinis

How to Infuse Your Own Spirits

Things You'll Need:

Liquor of choice

Glass bottle with a stopper that's slightly bigger than the liquid volume

Funnel

Strainer

Fruits, vegetables, peppers, herbs or spices

Step One

Choose your liquor, and begin thinking its intrinsic qualities. For example, gin is aromatic and floral, while rum tends to be smoky or spicy. Understanding its flavorings will help you decide what ingredients to infuse.

Step Two

Once you've decided which qualities you want to highlight, select the flavorings you want to add to the infusion. Remember that gin works well with lavender, citrus and cucumber, while rum lends itself to tropical fruits and mint. Vodka pairs with everything from hot peppers to pears, basil or pumpkin, and bourbon is a great match for peaches

Step Three

Clean and dry the bottle. Wash, dry and prepare the ingredients you plan to infuse. Depending on the amount of heat you want to impart, peppers can be left whole or cut. Likewise, the flavor of garlic will be more intense if it's sliced. Peel skin and/or pith from fruits and slice. Berries can be left whole.

Step Four

To infuse liquor, place ingredients in the prepared bottle, and pour the alcohol through a funnel, taking care to cover what's inside.

Step Five

Seal the bottle, and allow liquid to steep in a cool place, untouched for three days and up until two weeks. As a general rule of thumb, potent ingredients like citrus fruit, garlic, and hot peppers need to infuse for 3 to 5 days; fruits like pineapple, berries and honeydew benefit from a week or more time. Ditto with herbs.

Step Six

Test the flavor of the infused liquor every day, and add additional ingredients if necessary.

Step Seven

Once your infusion is ready, let creativity be your guide. Whether you opt to serve your drink on ice or up, strain the infused liquor before using it to make a beverage.

Rekindling the Kin Family Reunion

Party Theme Description

Celebrate life, treasured memories, enduring relationships, shared experiences and the unique bonds that have held families together.

Party Tips/ Planning Stages

Getting Started- Beginning with a phone or written survey is a great start! The survey is a great way to get some ideas of what when and where this event will take place. Once surveys are finished, you'll know how to proceed.

Planning- Form a committee to begin the planning process. It's a good idea to begin this process 12-18 months ahead. Early planning helps to secure a venue, funds for activities, etc.

The committee should have a strong leader who can be depended on in gaining momentum as the event approaches. Hosting a reunion is not a one person job! So gather your team together!

Meetings should be held at least twice a month if possible to coordinate efforts. It may also be a good idea to put together a website so other family members can track the progress of the reunion as well.

Type of Reunion- Consider what type of reunion you'd like to conduct. Two of the most popular choices are Picnics and Weekend events. Remember to include activities that are age appropriate and fun for all!

Set a Budget- Reunions can become very costly to put together, understanding where money is needed and how things will be paid for is instrumental. One person can not bear the load. Consider registration fees, this will help defray the cost of some expenses.

Party Tips/ Planning Stages (cont.)

- Fund-Raising Ideas
- Sell Raffle Tickets- prizes can be donated from area corporations
- Host A Bake Sale
- Host A Movie Night- get tickets at a discounted rate and up sale to raise monies for the reunion
- Host A Book Exchange- Pass on the gift of knowledge (see our Book Exchange Party*Print)
- Host A Skating Party
- Host A White Elephant Auction
- Host A Candlelight Bowling Party
- Sell Family Cookbooks

Party Activities

Family Heritage & Elders Tribute

Passing of the Torch

Baby Photo Contest

Create Your Family Tree Tee

Family Seminars & Workshops

- Viewing Our Past
- Chit & Chat
- Getting 2 Know You

Dessert Buffet

Party Theme Description	A decadent way to celebrate any occasion! The dessert buffet is like hosting a Sweets Tasting Party. Tell your guests to bring their sweet tooth and forget about the pounds for one day. They won't regret it!
Party Tips/ Planning Stages	For 16-24 guests plan to have 160 pastries, 8 bottles of wine,3 pots of coffee/tea/cocoa
	Set out a variety of serving dishes… different shapes, colors, textures, etc to make the décor exciting.
	Offer 3 types of teas, gourmet coffee and decadent hot chocolate. Un sure of what kind of wine. Stick to a simple sparkling wine.
	Set up the buffet table- place a couple of small platters or plates of assorted pastries around the buffet. Make the spread as decorative as possible.
Party Activities	The invitations should convey an old fashioned decadent charm. A great idea would be to create handmade invites on recipe cards.
	Ask guests to bring a copy of their favorite recipe, later you can compile the recipes into a creative keepsake cookbook.
Party Food Ideas	Brownies, Cookies, Miniature Cakes, Pies, Tarts & Pastries.
Party Drinks	Sparkling Juice and Sparkling Wines add a wonderful finish to these decadent delights.

SPRING IN BLOOM BRUNCH

Party Theme Description

Make it a special day! After a long winter of hibernating, spring poses the perfect time to reconnect with family and friends!

Party Activities

Conduct a White Elephant Auction, use the funds to sponsor a get-together later in the year around the summer or winter holidays.

Give each guest a journal and encourage them to start fresh and "Spring In Bloom" with a fresh approach to their home, work and spiritual life!

Party Food Ideas

Mimosa Mini Bar
Breakfast Strata
Cinnamon Coffee Crumb Cake
Fresh Fruit Medley
Lime Mint Melon Salad
Savory Wraps
Crumpets or Scones with Butter and Jam

Party Drinks

Cranberry-Vanilla Bean Mimosa

Cranberry Juice, chilled
Ice Cubes
1 vanilla bean
Sparkling Wine
Garnish: Sugar & Halved vanilla beans

Combine 2 c cranberry juice & ice in shaker, scrape in seeds of vanilla beans, shake well. Strain into champagne glasses fill halfway top with sparkling wine.

Rim glass w/ sugar. Garnish w/ vanilla bean.

Taste of Tunica

**Party Theme
Description**

Tunica is known for its all-you-can-eat buffets and gourmet dining, so in honor mark your memories of Tunica and host a night of fun and excitement.

Invitations:

- The invite is the first point of contact to get your guests in the mood—send out announcements with three playing cards and a poker chip glued to the front of each.

Décor:

**Party Tips/
Planning Stages**

- To create party atmosphere, echo the casino and card theme throughout the room's décor.
- Use red and black as your main colors, with hints of gold and silver to signify a big win.
- Roll each napkin and wrap with a fake dollar bill.
- Ask your dealers to wear candy-colored visors.
- Photocopy fake money and add your own picture to the bills. (Do not photocopy real dollar bills…it is a FELONY!)

**Party Tips/
Planning Stages
(cont.)**

Guest Keepsakes:

- Deck of Cards- Check your local casino… most give them for free.

- Pack party favors in fake money bags… include some chocolate coins

- Give each guest a cheat sheet that ranks the winning from best to worst.

Party Activities

Game Tables:

Texas Hold'Em

Spades Table

Roulette Table

Craps Table

Party Food Ideas

Fringe Benefits:

Spiced Mixed Nuts

Suit Shaped Sandwiches

Playing Card Shaped Cookies

Party Drinks

Texas Tea

½ oz. Vodka

½ oz. Gin

½ oz. Tequila

½ oz. Rum

½ oz. Triple Sec

¼ fill Sour Mix

fill Coke, Garnish with a lemon

G.E.M.S. Celebration

"Laughter is the closest distance between two people"
- Victor Borge

Party Theme Description

Celebrate sisterhood and honor those that have been instrumental in your life... mark the event by matching each honored guest to a gemstone that reflects their personality.

Party Tips/ Planning Stages

- Stick to a To-Do List- Keep a schedule to prepare for your event
- Serve Foods You've Tasted- Since this is a more upscale event hiring a caterer would not be a bad idea.
- Go for Abundance- Be prepared...make sure you have more than enough than not enough food and drinks
- Look for unique items that represent and are matched to the gemstone that represents your honored guest.

Party Activities

G.E.M.S. Rites of Passage- Prepare a heartfelt rites of passage to share with your honored guest… asking them to give to others the things they have given to you.

G.E.M.S. Gifts- Honor each guest with tokens of appreciation in the colors of the gemstone in which you feel they represent.

Party Food Ideas

Make this event as upscale as possible…. Catering recommended!
Stuffed Chicken Breast
Vegetable Medley
Garden Salad
Dinner Rolls
Miniature Dessert Buffet- with a variety of desserts
Chocolate Dipped Strawberry Tray

Party Drinks

Pearl Cosmopolitan

Fill mixing glass with ice.

3 ½ oz. Citrus Vodka
Dash Orange Liqueur
Dash Lime Juice
Dash White Cranberry Juice

Shake. Strain into chilled glass.

TAILGATER'S CHALLENGE

Party Theme Description

Whether you are a fan of the pigskin, make no mistake…tailgating is a great way to get family and friends together for the time of their lives… try tailgating with a twist! Challenge your guests to form teams and host the ultimate tailgating cook-off!

Choose a team captain for each team. You can have as many teams as you may want! The more the merrier, right?

On the invitation to the challenge, encourage guests to contact their team leader and think of a team name, colors, mascot, etc. Make sure team captains report this information back to you! This will allow you to coordinate space and décor to the teams theme.

Party Tips/ Planning Stages

Teams will be asked to prepare dishes in several different categories…you choose! For example, Appetizers, Entrée, Side Dishes & Dessert.

As the host of the challenge you should be prepared to provide each team the equipment needed to conduct the challenge. Teams will be responsible for food and ingredients.

Be weather conscious. Rain or Shine the game will go on ad so should the tailgating! It's not a bad idea to conduct this event under a tent.

Party Activities	Include some interactive & fun team activities. The more interactive the more the guests enjoy being a part of the fun!
Party Food & Drink Ideas	Be prepared for tailgating mishaps…Plan ahead and prepare foods that are known crowd pleasers for your guest to enjoy even while to challenge is being conducted.
Party Keepsakes	The winners of the challenge should all leave with a really nice keepsake…think about putting together miniature Styrofoam coolers filled with tailgating tools, snacks, drinks, etc. Make it as unique as possible!
	Give other participants a nice thank-you gift… think about giving each guest a long-handled grilling utensil or an apron that says " I was a participant in the 1st Annual Tailgating Challenge"
	Ideas for keepsakes for this type of event are unlimited!

Make Your Own

Commemorative Tailgater's 10

WOW! Your winners of your Tailgater's Challenge with a custom made Commemorative Tailgater's 10…

In your Tailgater's 10 include ten of the most memorable items that you know would leave the most impressive image in the minds of all of your guests.

1. Insulated Cooler

2. Stainless Steel BBQ Grilling Set

3. Collapsible Chair in Bag

4. Custom Labeled Bottle Water

5. Fingertip Towels in Team Colors

6. Reusable Plates, Cups & Plasticware in Team Colors

7. Your Favorite Tailgating Food Recipes

8. Your Favorite Tailgating Drink Recipes

9. Favorite Team Memorabilia

10. Thermos

Tailgater's Survival Kit

2 cutting boards
Chef's knife
4 mixing bowls
Serving Platters
Long-handled tongs & spatula for grill
Several large spoons
2 pots
Can opener
Paper Towels
Plastic Bags
Hand Sanitizer
Matches
Plastic bowls & eating utensils
2 coolers
2 large thermoses
Table
Folding Chairs
Sunscreen
Grill
Tabletop Burner

You Know You're A Tailgater When...

- You forget the tickets, but remember the ice!

- You stop by the stadium on an off day just to gaze at your favorite space!

- You can close your eyes and imagine a clear map of the location of the portable toilets in at least three different stadium parking lots.

- You have at least six beer mugs and a grill cover emblazoned with your favorite team's logo.

- You've cancelled/rescheduled an appointment because you realized it conflicted with a tailgate party!

SPAHHH! PARTY

Party Theme Description	Enjoy all of the amenities of a day spa in the privacy, comfort & convenience of your own home or location of your choice!
Party Tips/ Planning Stages	**Keepsakes** Give each guest a Spa @ Home take home gift bag complete with a shower gels, lotions, emery board, nail clipper, etc.
Party Activities	Mini Chair Massage Mini Foot Soak Mini Hand Exfoliation Mini Facials Intro to Pilates, Yoga, etc.
Party Food Ideas	Nothing is better than a day of relaxation topped off with a decadent spa buffet complete with… Fruit Platter Vegetable Platter Chicken or Turkey Wraps Mini Sandwiches Petit fours Orange Glazed Blueberry Scones

Mimosa
Sparkling Juice
Minted Pineapple Juice
Watermelon Nectar
Honeydew Fizzes

Party Drinks

Lemonade Caipirnhas

2 Large limes, cut into 16 wedges each
½ c sugar
6 c crushed ice
1 c store-bought lemonade
2 c cachaca (Brazilian Brandy)

Crush limes and sugar into a large measuring cup until juices are released, pour in cachaca. Transfer mixture to a large pitcher, and fill with ice. Stir in lemonade. Divide evenly among glasses. Garnish with lemon and lime slices, if desired.

A Father's Day

Party Theme Description

'Father's Day" will consist of mini seminars to help and embrace these young men who are in or approaching fatherhood. We are gearing up to help eradicate the "deadbeat dad" syndrome that seems to plague our community simply from fear of the unknown, so to speak.

Party Tips/ Planning Stages

- Ask for area organizations to assist in conducting mini seminars for the fathers to be.

- Ask area businesses to donate items that will be put into the Father's Day Diaper Bag.

- Invite young men that are father's to be and at-risk for "deadbeat dad" syndrome.

Party Activities

- Create A Baby Time Capsule- great for keeping photos and keepsakes

- Make Your Own Father's Day Survival Kit- complete with the things a father should have on the day of his child's birth

- Make a Personalized Baby Blanket

Party Food Ideas

Deluxe On the Go Lunches

- Complete with sandwich, cookies, fresh fruit cup and a soft drink.

Or A Hearty Hot Lunch

- Complete with Rich Man's Lasagna, Garlic Bread, Vegetable Medley or Salad and a Decadent Dessert Buffet.

Party for a Cause

Party Theme Description	Be an inspiration and the antidote to your community and those in need of support. Host a heartwarming event that allows you to give back in a big way!

First receive approval from the charity that you will be hosting the benefit for.

Answer a few key questions, what type of event are you planning? Are you proposing to obtain vendor-donated prizes for the event?

Party Tips/ Planning Stages — Coordinate a date with the event coordinator. Create a checklist of things you will need to do.

Prior to the event send a brief written description for the organization's newsletter.

Invite guests that support the cause. Introduce to others the cause in which you are planning the event.

Host a silent auction of items that have been received as donations.

Party Activities — Make sure you don't forget your guest. Have fun icebreakers, door prizes that will make the event memorable.

Party Food Ideas

You have so many choices here. You could literally have a formal dinner or a food fete of hors'. Unlimited options! Consider having a menu that ties your theme together.

Party Drinks

From wines to classic cocktails your party for a cause can offer some very unique drinks! Again consider tying your drinks to your theme.

"Get Active" Challenge

Party Theme Description	A monthly monitored 6-month "Get Active" event guaranteed to help you think about and then change the way you live. It is a mission to Re-invent a new you! The "New Beginnings, New Plateau, New You….Get Active" Challenge encourages all participants to become more healthy in mind, body and spirit!
Party Tips/ Planning Stages	Over the course of the 6-month challenge participants will attend monthly *Celebrate You Checkpoints.* Make these checkpoints fun and interactive by offering health screenings, fitness demos, door prizes, drawings, on the spot challenges, freebies and more! Each guest pays an agreed upon amount of money to participate. The money is put into a pool that will be awarded to the biggest loser in the challenge.

	Checkpoints	
	Month One	
	Kick-off	1st Weigh In
	Month Two	
	Heart Healthy Brunch	2nd Weigh In
Party Activities	Month Three	
	Extreme Fitness Challenge	3rd Weigh In
	Month Four	
	Double Up Challenge	4th Weigh In
	Month Five	
	Over the Hump Pamper Party	5th Weigh In
	Month Six	
	Get Active Celebration	6th Weigh In
Party Keepsakes	Get Active Drawstring Bag filled with participant T-shirt, Custom labeled bottle water, pedometer, a journal, CD of great workout music.	

Hosting A Speed Networking Social

Party Theme Description

Fun, exciting and effective way to make a lot of initial connections in a very different environment from the standard business networking meetings. Speed networking programs are showing up all around the world.

Party Tips/ Planning Stages

- Give each guest short intervals to meet each other.
- Have a bell that will ring when it is time for each guest to move on to the next person.
- Individuals should sit across from one another and after the set time period.
- Allow guests 2-3 minutes to exchange information.

Tips

Start with the end in mind. Remember that you are there to find ways to connect with each and every person that you meet.

Conduct the speed networking as a mini interview. Try to find out as much as you can in the time you are allowed.

Making notes during the speed networking.

Follow up. If you don't follow up with those you have met, you will have only succeeded in wasting your time.

Set appointments with each person, with the intention of becoming better acquainted.

Tips & Tricks to Party like a PRO

Your turn to host a party but you don't know where to start? Pour a glass of wine, sit down and peruse our Party*Prints. From elegant and intimate to lively and exciting, we have a party plan for you... complete with details to help you not only host but enjoy the party as well.

Parties are such a fun way to share time with friends, meet new people and make your weekends memorable. Need a creative twist to a party idea? Try our *Make Your Own Martini Party.*

Invite friends for dinner, use our Last Minute Dinner Party plans. Check out our Good Luck Party for someone moving, taking a new job or getting married. Super Bowl means super party time, find out how with our Super Bowl Party plans. Throw your own movie celebration with our Oscar Night Party.

Party Etiquette

Always RSVP that you will/will not attend the meeting, conference, dinner, and never bring extra guests without first checking with the hosts or the planning committee.

- Be on time.

- Turn your cell phone off.

- Allow others to speak.

- Listen carefully to what is being said.

- Ask your question, if it has not already been answered.

- Keep questions relevant to the subject.

- Do not make people repeat themselves.

- Be courteous and thoughtful of those around you, regardless of the situation.

- Give others a chance to express concerns or problems they may have with an agenda item.

- Always talk in the vernacular of the industry and be clear without being condescending.

- Remember to use "please" and "thank you".

Party Planning Tips

When I plan a event, organization and preparation are critical to its' success. I pride myself on doing this in a timely fashion... descent and in order.

When planning an event for a client, I first take a look at the "Why" as there are numerous reasons to entertain. Once we have concluded on the why, we begin the process by creating an customized event bible. I have been blessed with the ability to create theme events off the top of my head that are creative and totally unique to my clients and their guests.

The following are suggestions; you decide how you want to entertain.

TYPE OF THEME: Denim & Diamonds, The Social Butterfly Girls Night Out, For the Love of Money Casino Night

DATE/TIME: Anytime is a great time to create memories!

LOCATION: You choose

GUEST LIST: However many guests you are comfortable inviting, If new at entertaining, start small.

INVITATION: E-mail, phone calls or in person.. I love to be creative and use a really nice unique theme inspired invitation.

MENU: Be creative and festive on your own or try catering the event.

DECORATIONS: Be creative, festive and mind-boggling! Try using things you already have and things that can be creatively displayed for added ambiance.

ORGANIZE PARTY DETAILS: Think your event through and create a list of what you need to do.

SHOPPING LIST: List all you need to buy, both food and supplies.

SCHEDULE OF TASKS: Organize a list of what needs to be done and when..

LOGISTICS: Understand your guests needs and plan for them.

TRAFFIC FLOW: Plan where you will place everything and how guests will get there.

Make Your Event More Than A Memory

You know what they say about first impressions. This is particularly true for an event and the event planner. This is the reason that we pride ourselves on creating the most memorable events. From concept to completion, MTM Events creates the greatest impact with decorating and theme planning. From the entrance to the exit we aim to create a festive mood for your guests.

No need to be overpriced and extravagant, just creatively smart. A MTM Event proves simple as color can create a theme.

I recently hosted a Girls Night Out for a local magazine. I themed the event "Paint the Town Red" to let the women in attendance know that the idea is that we, from time to time need to let our hair down and a let the good times roll! I filled paint cans with all kinds of unique red colored items, including perfume samples, nail polish, body butter samples, mini manicure sets, miniature bottles of sparkling theme together coupled with the pampering and keepsakes made this event More than A Memory!

BIBLIOGRAPHY

MTM Events would like to give credit to their most admired resources for creating the most fabulous cutting edge events.

The Party Goddess, Online, 10 July 2005. <http:www.partygoddess. com>

Godiva Chocolatier, Chocolate Trivia, Online, 3, January 2008. <http:// www.godiva.com/recipes/chocolate_trivia.aspx>

"Fun with Fondue". Sam's Club Source. February 2005. Volume 1, pg.26.

Love to Know, Christmas Wine Pairings, Online. 30, November 2007. <http://wine.lovetoknow.com/wiki/Christmas_Dinner_Wine_ Pairings>

"Holiday Party A Good Time Guide". A Change of Address. December 2007. Pg. 26

"How to Pull Off a Tailgate Party". Successful Promotions. September 2007. Pg 26.

NICOLE GATES is a native of Joliet, IL. She is the single mother of Yolanda, Savanna, and twins Brooklyn & Bheanna. Nicole is passionate so passionate about event planning that she took the extra steps to become a Certified Event & Meeting Planner and Theme Event Expert. Nicole's passion for planning events help her launch *Epiphany Marketing* which hosts seminars for Small Business Owners in the areas of ***Branding, Marketing, The Art of being Cordial-Customer Service, Dare 2 Dream- Living What U Love!*** Concepts and beliefs that she loves and has become her personal mantra!

So if *JOY* is the feeling of grinning on the inside… then I have been in a joyous state since the age of 18! It has always been my hearts desire to gather family, friends and my community for a fun time embraced by a memorable theme.

Nicole finally found her life's calling and passion in the form of Hospitality. She came to admire the creativity of David Tutera and Kathy Riva two well-known event planners. Their flair for creating cutting edge events inspired her to become an event planner and not only create cutting-edge events, but theme events! Tying the event all together gives her instant gratification, always able to see the end result in her mind. Her keen sense of coordinating the menu and keepsakes to the theme, the theme to the décor and invitations, has her clients excited and eagerly anticipating her next event.

Nicole believes that everyday she's living her life's dream! Being an event planner gives her unspeakable joy! In 2002 she started More Than A Memory Event Planners, where we began to create events for private and corporate clients. MTM has created signature events like the ***Retro Cocktail Party, Sunset Safari Party, Stress Less Fest, and The Essence Of Esther Day- a full-service Pamper Party*** for many elated clients.